M000313023

Heaven
In Our Hearts

Selected Poems by

Nick LeForce

Inner Works
Oroville, California
2012

Published by:

Inner Works
939 18th St.
Oroville, California 95965

ISBN: 978-0-9821166-9-2

Cover Art by: Tri Widyatmaka
Inside Illustrations by Junlin Chen

Dedication

To my mother, Vida Louise LeForce,
in loving memory.
Vida means "beloved" in Hebrew and "life" in Spanish
and she blessed me with this beloved life,
for which I am eternally grateful.

Heaven In Our Hearts

Introduction

I have been a part–time poet. Perhaps this is why the goddess of poetry is a fickle mistress who has blessed me with her presence often at inopportune times. "Perfect" words for a line of poetry pop into my mind in the middle of a meeting or while merging into traffic on a busy freeway. I capture what I can because I know she will play hide and seek with me when I sit to write.

I am grateful for the gifts she gives. I pay homage to her by playing with words, by sensing the shapes of sounds, and by peering into the scenes she offers as metaphors. On rare occasions, she rewards me with a whole poem in one piece. These are blessed moments. The poem, Heaven, was gifted to me in this way and the final line of that poem serves as the title for this collection. More often, writing poetry, for me, is a matter of working with the seed of an idea, letting it germinate, and watering it, even when unseen, in the hopes it will flourish. And those that do mature still require pruning and shaping.

I often tell people that one out of five poems will be decent, and one out of five decent poems will be good, and one out of five good poems will be really good. By really good I mean that I think the piece could stand up in the world of poetry. These are averages so I can't count on that fifth one coming through. After all, she is a fickle mistress!

This book is a collection of poems sifted out of seven books of poetry that I have produced over the past 10 years. Most of the poems in this set are decent, some are good, and a few are really good. I have read some at my personal development seminars on many occasions and they have been well received. But the joy of poetry is a matter of taste and I leave you to judge the quality of these works for yourself.

I strive to write from the heart based on my own personal experience while also expressing something more universal in the human condition. Specific people and events in my life provided inspiration for many of these poems. Consequently, some poems will make more sense when the context or event is understood. I have included a notes section at the end of the book to give interested readers the background and context, and to acknowledge sources, where I thought it might be helpful.

The poems are divided into four sections—Living, Losing, Learning, and Loving. Although this sequence is not mandatory, it may serve as a path. If we can use our living and losing as a learning to be more loving, then we do have a chance of finding heaven in our hearts.

The placement of poems in each section, though deliberate, is often arbitrary, and some poems could easily fit in more than one section. Perhaps it is appropriate that the boundaries between living, losing, learning, and loving may blur and one may well become another.

Living

The Seed of Life

Just before those first
rays of sunlight appear
on the horizon
you can feel the night
longing for the day.

It is raw and simple
like life confined
to a seed waiting
for the right time
to burst forth.

The seed of life in you
needs that dark place
to grow into a yearning
the husk cannot hold.

Until,
no matter how hard
your shell, it will crack
open to the light coming
from beyond
your own horizon.

Without A Map

Every tree knows
        that to stand tall,
        you must send your roots deep
            finding soil even in the crevices
            between solid rock.

Every bear knows
        how to dream of the spring
        in that long winter of hibernation
            without calendars or clocks
            even after months
            and fifteen feet of snow covering the den.

Every bird knows
        just when to migrate,
        just where to fly
            without a map,
            without even a memory
            of the place and yet

the tree does grow,
the bear does dream,
the bird does fly.

Money

Is it not just a piece of paper?
Recycled rag and processed pulp
the bark of a once living tree
stamped with a new life
in print and patterns
and colored green with envy
because it always wants
to be something else.

It knows it is useless in itself
a fragile ego made whole
only when it is honored
by the masses
when it passes through
a thousand hands
in exchange for something
of real value
or when it is stored
in the vaulted temples
and its unseen presence tallied
as a measure of a person's
net worth.

We give it this authority.
Yet its very life depends on us.
It is nothing without us
but a piece of paper
we have come to worship.

Do not be deceived.
Remember, always,
the true power of money
lives inside of you.

Armchair Adventurer

Even the armchair adventurer
will one day come home
bearing maps of lands unknown,
of places no one else can go;
shoe–worn and travel weary,
telling stories no one hears
and no one sees the sadness
from all the years
of living life on the sidelines.

If only promises,
inked on parchment and
tucked onto dusty shelves,
could show the way;
could bind us to the spine,
opening pages filled
with the loves and losses;
the misery and magnificence
of a ragtag team of misfits
you can only come to love
over time.

If only we could let our lives
become a page–turner,
every part of the plot
a piece of a puzzle
that adds up to something
you cannot wait to discover.

If you read between the lives
of every armchair adventurer,
you will see someone
longing to live a life
that cannot be put down;
a life to which you want to return
in every waking moment
all the way through
to the end.

Sky in a Jar

How I wish to capture the sky in a jar
and hold it out to you as Hannah did.

She knows the quivering you feel
when someone traces the fault line
across your soul
and can take you back
to the time
when the old world
and the new world
were still one continent.

She wears the years like a scarf
draped around her neck
clothes color–coordinated
and stands in perfect politeness.
But she still feels her own nakedness,
still savors succulent blackberries
hand–picked so the juice stains her fingers
eating only the ripest, those bursting with life,
because she knows
even caged animals
weep for their dead.

She dazzles those, like me,
who walk with silk crutches
taunting us to throw them aside
to dance with her across the rainbow
filling an open jar
with the heavens.

I went out that very night
and began shooting stars
at the moon
and I felt contented
even though
every single one
missed the mark.

Cup of Life

We cannot stop it—
no matter how great the wall
or how deep the moat.
We cannot keep the world
outside of ourselves.

The cup of life has no end
offering itself
bitter, sweet, and beautiful.
How can we learn
to bear such happiness?

Our bodies are too small,
our minds too narrow,
our years too short
to hold this moment.

Let us take our sip
and live life
overwhelmed.

Let's Go

Let's go, you and I, let's go.

Let's go pluck stars from the heavens
and toss them like skipping stones
across the surface of our lives.

Let's go nestle in the soft wing feathers
of a goose and migrate
to the warmer places in our hearts.

Let's go linger in lounge chairs
on an ancient Martian seabed
and count satellites circling the earth.

Let's go ride an electric current
through all the switches in our soul
until we see the light.

Let's go sing whale songs
to each other
across the oceans that separate us.

Let's go run away
to the sacred places inside ourselves
where we have always lived
and share all the secrets
we never before dared speak.

Let's go, you and I, let's go.

Moon Lake

We never seem to have enough time
for two goals and a hundred pairs of shoes.
Both directions fill us with fear and desire
and we find ourselves approaching and avoiding
what we most want
neither enjoying the heights
nor experiencing the depths.

Instead, we set our sights on incense and a BMW
though we know the book of the future
will remain unwritten
until we shed a lake of tears
for all the times we lacked courage
or did not believe in ourselves
enough to say, "I love you."

But once we decorate our lives
in ways that please us;
once we sit with ourselves sipping tea,
we will know we have found
the one teacher
who can give us back our hearts.

Then, we can put on our hiking boots.
We can take our loved ones
to the mountain lake during a full moon
and say, "I give you this beauty.
But the life under the surface is my own."

Memories

Memories wrapped in gift boxes.
The fragrance of flowers
and last night's dreams.
The colors of love quietly
painted across the walls.

We stand in the shadow of a promise
watching words escape us
as if fleeing from the moment.
They must make it
all the way around the world
before coming back to us;
before our hearts can receive them.

We dare not open these gifts
in front of each other.
We fear we hope for too much.
And even though we won't admit it,
we fear there is too much longing
and too much beauty in the world
for us to be seen.

But our eyes are not deceived.
The arched pathway
we open to each other
hangs with trumpet vine and jasmine.
We only need to follow
where our feet go
and the gifts will open themselves.

What Lives In Us

We cannot change our history.
What parts us in our heritage
does not part us in spirit.
I see my face in your face,
hear my voice in your voice,
feel my sorrow in your sadness
and my joy in your jubilance.

What lives in you, lives in me.

The flesh, meat, and bone
that houses us
suffers our abuse,
withstands our indignities,
and follows our bidding.

But we can't deny life.

We are moved by forces
we cannot fathom.
We cry when hurt,
bleed when cut.
But what leaks from us
does not diminish us.

We cannot contain life.

What lives in me, lives in you.

Ocean of Life

The ocean of life calls us back,
again and again,
rumbling waves upon our shore;
crumbling nanoseconds into sand...

Children dance dodging waves—
Splash–happy moments;
sun–sleepy memories
come and go with the tides
and the turning of earth and moon
by forces we cannot see; cannot capture

through the lens of a camera—still, moving—
the moments come over us, again and
again, waves and tides
and time enough to know
why we are here and what we live for
crumbling into sand
in rhythms that remind us

we will be taken back
into the ocean
collected,
consumed,
completed.

Fascination

Fascination abandoned his petition for entry into heaven
because he did not want to follow the rules
or wait for his cue. Instead, he fell to the earth
burning northern lights across the sky
and painting the red–orange hues of sunset.
He sprinkled glittering points of light
across the ocean under a full moon
arriving to sing love songs with a ukulele
under the balcony for you. He was courted
by movie moguls and artisans
all wishing to be blessed with his fortune.
Yet he loves the downtrodden
and will give no less to them.

I met him at a coffee shop with his sister,
Enchantment, and let him bend my ear with his stories.
I had to pull myself away
compelled to meet the demands of the day.
He tossed me a coin as I walked out.
I watched the arc of silver flashing across the room
tumbling upon itself, knocking the light into my eyes
again and again; my hand lifting on its own,
catching it at arc end…

and the light shone in me for days.

Looking Fate in the Face

A casual conversation plants seeds,
sparks an interest,
spurs us in search of something
we had no desire for
or knowledge of beforehand.

We may never know
how much of our lives
are a matter of being
in this place, at this time.

A future best friend
may be sitting next to you
in a room full of strangers.

We do not know when
we are looking fate in the face.
The future is woven into our present
in patterns we cannot see
and do not control:
choice and chance and happenstance
and lives lived in the balance.
Somewhere between
what we are given
and how we are taken,
our hearts will turn,
and our minds will move,
without our knowing.

Life always offers itself fully.
But you can only take
what you are willing to give.

Forever Etched

Only when the years have whitewashed your hair;
Only when life has etched itself upon your face;
Only then will you come to yourself whole.

Only when you have loved, and lost, and loved again;
Only when you have traveled down dead end roads
And left a thousand projects unfinished;
Only then will you come to yourself whole.

Only when you have embraced the other face
of your two–faced life;
Only when you have slept in the bed of your own lies;
Only then will you come to yourself whole.

Only when the wind and water have weathered the edges of you;
So much so that you are a remnant of what you once were;
Only then will you come to yourself whole.

Not as arms and legs.
Not as thoughts and feelings,
Not as deeds and accomplishments,
But as something wholly unknowable.

Only then will you find your Self
Forever etched upon the face of the universe.

Nick LeForce

Losing

The Invitation

The invitation will come
in the form of chaos—
patterns interrupted;
routines disrupted.
As a dying man in the desert
no longer cares for timecards
or morning coffee,
you are bound to let go
of whatever you cling to.

The invitation will come
when you let
your fields go fallow
and you become
the seedless vessel
because only emptiness
can contain the universe.

The invitation will come
when all doors open into darkness
and you enter rooms without a future
knowing the only thing left to find
is yourself. Acceptance

requires more than "Yes."
It grows out of your life
and beyond you
into your dreams
coloring what you may become—
what has always been
cocooned within you
waiting to be released.

Half–Life

We were not meant
to live a half–life of the soul
or to beg forgiveness
for the mistake of entering the world.

We may come to know ourselves
as we are seen,
but the face
behind the mask
is without sin.

Now we can go back
before we were convicted.
We can undo all the years
of self–imposed exile.

We can let go of our stories.
They are wounded birds
we have nursed
all these years
and have come to love.

But they do not belong in cages—
Dreams do not live behind bars.
We must set them free
because only the hollow heart
is eager to be filled.

Innocence

Some know the exact moment innocence was ousted.
They can name the tragedy that ended childhood
or date the initiation into a grown–up world.
For me, it is not so easy. The lines blurred
living, as I did, outside my body and spirit broken—
unwilling to face the bullies
but willing to bear the whipping.
Rather than lose a losing battle,
I battled, instead, losing face.

But now, I know, saving face is not what matters.

I know what renders the heart happy.
And it won't be found
in fat savings accounts
or fine new cars;
it can't be worn around the neck
or won in battle.
What renders the heart happy
is found in memories of moments without end
swimming in the ocean of your eyes
or surfing the waves of your laughter.

Perhaps it is a sad soul seeking redemption
that believes a few moments loving amount to more
than all the mistakes and misgivings;
that what is truly human in us
can lift us out of our limitations;
that we, mere mortals, can glimpse heaven
in the face of the beloved
and find, once again,
a sweet innocence
living within.

Misplaced Moments

I have elevated the act
of misplacing items
to a fine art

as if there is within me
a devious adolescent
playing a prank on a friend

by hiding
that one piece of paper,
that one set of keys,
that one little bit of importance

and then watching
with amusement
as I look for it frantically.

I do not want to know
how much time I've spent
in those misplaced moments
searching for something
I know to be where it is not
because it *was* there a minute ago.

I do not want to know
how often I've retraced my steps
redone my work
re–searched my soul

trying to find the patron saint
of the lost and found
who can lift a box
of forgotten treasures
and mislaid trinkets

from behind a counter
where I may find
what I have been looking for
and, with a mix of gratitude and relief,
say "thank you,"
"thank you,"
"thank you."

Clay

I read words in a book
that changed me once.

I remember feeling
the soil of my soul
turning over ready
to receive new seed.

I remember wondering
if it were the clay from which
God fashioned Adam.

I did not highlight the text
or underline the words.

I did not dog–ear the page
where this wisdom lived.

And the words faded from memory.

I have since looked back
over countless pages,
reread entire books searching
for words that will sink
deep into my being
and germinate life.

I have learned
that words are just a container
like the dog–eared pages that hold them.

They are nothing but the shell
that must crack open within you.

What matters is the life
that grows out of them
from soil worked with your own hands
until the dirt stains your fingers;
watered with your own tears
for what you have left buried
deep within you.

Weightlessness

Einstein taught us
what we already know:
that you and I
see our own truths
accurately.
He proved the equivalence
of gravity and acceleration
though pulling down
and moving on
do not feel the same
to me.

I have not known
the weightlessness
of interstellar space.
But I do feel the loneliness traveling
between planets and stars
and the eerie sensation
of space and time curving around me;
or how so many moments pass by
near the speed of light
and the one I see in the mirror
every day
ages so much more quickly than I.

Still, I remain
pinned to the earth;
held by a love
more powerful
than all the equations describing
bodies in motion
and the laws of attraction.

Every leap
brings me back
to where I started
pulling down and moving on
my own weightless truth,
which is always right here—
until I hold it,
and then it belongs
to Einstein and every one
other than me.

The White Stick

I watched you suck the world in
through the white stick,
the lover you carry in your pocket
and pay for with your dreams.

It funnels the fire you long to hold in your hand,
the fire you long to ignite in your breast.
It grants you passage to the secret places
where friends read each other's fortunes.

I heard you rail against the white stick,
whose silence bears all your rage
and on whose presence you have come to depend.

The lover you have left and come back to
over and over again; the lover who will
in the end, take your breath away.

Struggling to Relax

We carry the weight
of a dark world
in tensed muscles,
and tight jaws.

Struggling to relax
against what we bear
in our bodies.

Without knowing
our eyes were made
to look out on a world
we must learn to live in
and not back at ourselves
where we fear there is no light.

We are too close to see
it is our own sun blinding us.

We are too foolish to know
we are clinging to nothing.

Always in the emptying
we will find what we did not know
we were looking for.
We cannot carry the world
we live in. But we can learn
to let the world carry us.

The Reservoir of Sadness

We know better
        than to take
        that narrow, lonely path
        through the woods.
        The one never walked
        yet so well trodden.

We know better
        than to go
        to that black sand beach
        at the edge
        of the reservoir
        of sadness.

            A place better left as it is.
            A matter better kept taboo.

Because we know
        our homes were sacrificed there.

We know
        our loved ones drowned there.

We know
        sacred ground is buried there
        under the water.

But now,
>we have come
>out of the coma
>>where we hovered
>>through the years
>>between life and death
>>unwilling to choose either.

>Unaware that each time
>we did not choose
>added another stone to the wall;
>keeping the lowlands safe
>from periodic floods
>by a dam
>we did not know we built.

We find ourselves
>awakened here
>sitting on the black sand beach
>where the depths call us back.
>Back into the coma.

We know
>the water will take us
>as no one else has—
>whole, complete
>nothing held back.

We know
>we must go naked
>into the water
>because whatever we wear
>will weigh us down,
>>down,
>>>down.

And we will sink
      into our sadness
      and our sanity;
      into the comfort
      of our coma.

Awakened now
      we see other choices.

We know
      we are not here
      to take the dive,
      but to pay homage
      to all that is unknown in us.

And then to walk
      the never–walked path
      out of the woods,
      out of hiding,

choosing,
      for the first time,
      to live.

Freedom

I love you like a caged animal loves the beauty of the world.
You are the land where what's wild in me lives;
the home where I belong.

I awaken each morning eyes filled
with the last sight of you,
heart dancing between
danger and delight in your embrace.
With you, nothing in life is barred,
all things may come and go.

I long for the key
that will open me to you again,
afraid I have lived life locked
too long to step through the door
and I know I can always love you
from the inside, safely,
like a caged animal loves the beauty of the world.

Rhythms of the Heart

Are you willing to follow
the rhythms of the heart—
to go where it will take you?
Even if you must be blindfolded
so that you will not know the way
to the secret hideouts
of outcasts and rebels
who live within you?
Even if it asks you
to join in a cause
that puts you at odds
with a world you have come to love?

Are you willing to follow
the rhythms of the heart—
to go where it will take you?
Even if it requires you to strip naked
and walk before judging eyes
back to the tree of knowledge?
Even if you risk exile
because your heart knows
whether or not
you have become
a traitor to your own life?

Are you willing to follow
the rhythms of the heart—
to go where it will take you?
Even if you must stop your life
long enough to feel
the slow, deliberate growth of trees
bending toward the sun?

Even if it melts you
into every shifting shade of color
in a sunset's horizon and then
pours you through baby laughter
out into the world again?

Are you willing to follow
the rhythms of the heart—
to go where it will take you?
Even if it calls you to arise before dawn
and skate across the thin ice that covers
the crack between the worlds?
Even if you must ride the storm to Oz
and complete the tasks
the wizard gives you
in order to claim
what is already yours?

Are you willing to follow
the rhythms of the heart—
to go where it will take you?
Even if it asks you to dance
in your crippled body clumsily
right out loud for all to see
because your heart knows
life does not care
for your handicaps
but does care
that you give your all.

Are you willing now
to follow the rhythms of the heart?

Generations

Every generation must bury
its mothers and fathers
or we will carry the weight
of their dreams and disappointments
to our own grave.

But we can create an altar to our ancestors—
give them a place of honor
that holds the space they fill in our lives.

We can bring them flowers and food
on the day of the dead
and let our tears
water the ground where they rest.

Because we know there is a time
for every creature to be called home.

And even though they gave us life,
a debt we can never repay,
we must turn away from their shadow
and face our own sun.

We must feel our own disappointments
and follow our own dreams.

And we must do our best
to free our children
of the chains that hold us

because every generation must bury
its mothers and fathers
and we, too, shall one day
be called home.

Ourselves

We remain ourselves
though we do not know
what we contain.
Our bodies are made
over and over again
with anonymous atoms.

We are bearers of stardust
and elephant dung.

Ancient winds blow through us—
whispers we can feel in our bones
and almost know in those nights
we are beyond sleep
when stillness lets us feel
a million unseen particles
leaping out into oblivion.

This truth slumbers
throughout our lives.
Yet, it is everywhere
around us, in us,
passing through us.

We give ourselves
to the universe
to be made new,
over and over again,
and we never know it
because we remain
ourselves.

Down to the Bone

Picking at it over and over again,
wondering: will it end at thigh or rib?
Or something without a name—
a missing link in a line
that leads back to apes and to angels.
And, once found, fills the gaps, answers all the questions
that we have chewed on for years.

I tell myself over and over again,
"I have no need of these things."
No need to count sheets through the shredder
or bags full of memories put in garbage bins
or trunk–filled trips to Goodwill,
though every item held a piece of me
hostage, abandoned. Scattered now to the world—

the ashes of loved ones finally freed.

At last laying the past to rest
for we have lives to live and life
will pick at us over and over again
until we feel it clean through to the bone
and know ourselves as apes and as angels
and as something without a name.

Learning

The Shipwrecked Soul

Beware the captain
    That sails only on smooth waters;
    That drops anchor only in safe harbors;
    That lets aboard only familiar faces;
    That will not brook strong winds or stormy weather;

Whose life, well lived, is a deadly comfort—
    Never to be dashed against the rocks of passion
    Never to be dismembered on the shores of love.

Yet a life so well lived it hides a shipwrecked soul.

I have been such a captain.

But now I set out on unknown seas

With sails full open
    Guided only by whispers in the wind;
    By images in white capped waves;
    By patterns in the flight of birds;
    And by bits of news from distant ports;

In search of that soul survivor,
The almost forgotten fragments of Self
That shall heal the world as the world heals me.

Fate

Fate is a harsh master
sparking a fire for each other
in the hearts of two people
who cannot be together;
birthing an unwanted baby
to a mother incapable of love;
bringing friends who play foul
and betray the deepest trust.

It's no wonder we harbor
a hatred we cannot put down,
we hold on to a hurt
that defines who we are.

It's no wonder we're afraid
to take center position
in our own lives,
choosing, instead,
to be on the sideline
and longing for a freedom
that's just out of reach.

It's no wonder we lay our troubles
at the feet of our teachers
who tell us that we can have
the beach house of our dreams,
that we can walk
in a garden of endless flowers;
that we can build
a rainbow bridge
between the world we wake to
and the world we dream.

But in the end it's still up to us
to make the tough choices
at the crossroads we come to
and to face our fate as a mirror
showing outside us what is within.

Only then can we puzzle the pieces together;
only then can we sit at the center of our lives.

Dancing with Shadows

I will fail you.
You will fail me.
Perhaps each day little by little
or all at once becoming no more
than the mere shadow of a fantasy—
insubstantial—falling short,
flat–angled, changing
with the arc of sunlight
until disappearing into night.

How heavy the weightless fall?
Sticking to ground where
no arms can lift us.
How loud the muted thud?
Falling in the forest
where no ears can hear us.

And the pain will echo
across the widening canyon
between us. While deep below
a river flows from tears shed
for the loss of what we never had.

Yes, I will fail you.
And you will fail me.
Little by little or all at once,
and over and over again,
until we learn to dance
with each other's shadow
and complete ourselves
in the world we create.

Stories

You can give me
all the reasons
why you came
and they will not account for
why you are here.

There is more life
in "once upon a time"
than in all the logic
of the last five thousand years.

I will never know you
by your name
or occupation.
I will never know you
by your degrees
or your income.

I will only know *you*
by the stories of
what has shaped your soul;
what moves you
through your days
and what dreams
you hold precious.

So come,
       sit with me.

Tell me the tales
of the wars
       you have waged;

the hearts
      you have broken;

the loves
      you have lost;

the lessons
      you have learned;

the trials and triumphs in a life lived
as only you can live it;
told as only you can tell it.

?

The question mark, ?:
an inverted hook hanging over a period
of time it takes to dive into wonder.

The lure is in the line before the hook
because the hook does not snag you.

Instead, it lifts you up
and turns you back into yourself.

It offers the freedom
to go as far as you can
and as deep as you wish.

With the patience of a saint,
it waits for your return, waits
for you to bring back the treasures
that can only be found under the surface.

The best askermen bait the line carefully
tilting everything toward the hook that will
turn you inside and wonder to themselves:

Who will take the dive?
How deep will you go?
What jewels will you find there?

Message in a Bottle

Never ask a poet for advice
unless you are willing to tolerate ambiguity
because a poet speaks in more than meaning,
wraps words in rhythms, sounds in sensations;

giving you, instead, a message in a bottle
tossed in the sea from a distant shore,
written in a code you must crack
and filled with the fragments of a map
that may just lead you to the treasure
your heart most desires;

it's a code you can only crack
when you are willing to love life
with all its longing and let down,
its empty passions and broken promises,
its endless tomorrows flowing into today;

and a treasure you can only claim
when you are willing to embrace
the struggles that make you strong,
to fight the battles that make you brave,
to show the weakness that inspires your wisdom;

all acts of courage no advice can contain;
and the poet will tell you,
"don't bottle your dreams,
don't let them drift to other shores,"
because dreams are seeds and precious things,

they do no good held in the hand,
they need the land and the love
of one who knows that the seed
looks nothing like the tree it will become.

Trees

I want the deep sleep of trees
that can dream for weeks and months
undisturbed by wind and storms
rooted as they are in life
and growing rings each year
around a question
they do not need to answer.
Knowing themselves
not by what they say or do,
but by drinking sunlight,
caressing earth,
kissing heaven,
and holding fast to a truth
that can only be found
by one who is willing
to stand still
through the passing of seasons
year after year.

Precious Mettle

Lives in limbo at 30,000 feet—
living shy of our purpose
in a world ruled by fear.
Knowing our wings cannot keep us from the earth
because we are miners more than aviators.

We know we must sift through
the silt and sediment of our lives
to find the precious nuggets.

We must strip a mountain of false bravado
to find the ore of our true mettle.

We must wade out into waters
where we cannot be baptized,
present the self that cannot be saved,
to awaken what has been silenced in us for years.

And then we come to know,
for the first time,
that we are enough;
that we each have,
in our own small way,
something to offer this world.

That gift, when given, is our salvation;
and it will take us closer to heaven
than our wings can ever go.

Twists and Turns

I may never know
the twists and turns
you have taken
on your path.

I may never know
the dark nights
of your soul
or the irritants
that sourced your pearls.

I may never know
the turmoil
you have endured
or the bliss
you have embraced
to become who you are.

But I do know
these unknown parts of you,
twisted and turned
in the great wheel of life,
allowed you to lead me now
to the gates of the garden.

For through you
I have learned
to embrace the turmoil,
to endure even the bliss
of my life,
as I work the irritants
into pearls of my own.

And you may never know
the gratitude I feel
for the gifts you have given
because it cannot be conveyed
in a hug
or contained
in a "thank you."

But it will go with me
on all the twists and turns
of my own path
and it will grow with me
through all the years to come
in the garden
of my becoming.

Resurrected Dream

What comes of coins
tossed in the fountain of wishes
when we turn away from the well
in order to live in a world
that does not dream?

It is easy to let
the death of a dream
go unnoticed
first feeling out of reach
fading, slipping away
into dark recesses
neglected forgotten
until one day it is gone

And where do dead dreams go?
what ancient burial ground
holds the bones of our desire?
what little bits of ourselves
did we bury there
to guide the dead to heaven?

Then one day
A flash catches the corner of our eye
a glittering reflection of long ago light
striking a coin left forgotten
sparking life like a genie
out of the lantern and
the resurrected dream rises up

right out of the pain of the past,
the seemingly meaningless moments,
the detours and dead ends
now become milestones and markers,
necessary steps on a journey
we did not know we were taking,
following a path
we did not know was leading us
right to where we are now
where we sit and watch
the sun set on the past
and the sun rise on the future

Sacred Relics

I do not know when
I lost my footing on the earth
or when I moved upstairs
from the heart to the lofty places
where ideas dance.
I do not know how many steps
I must take to make the pilgrimage
back to the holy land.

But I do know the longing
for something that cannot be named;
the missing of something unknown
as if the day calls me;
calls me out to play…

because I was once eager
to go outside.

I once knocked on the doors of friends
uninvited.

I once moved in my body
as if I belonged there.

But here I am, now,
in the middle of my life,
with duties to be done
and chores to be completed

while the pilgrim comes, uninvited,
knocking at the door of my heart;
bringing sacred relics
of the life I have not yet lived;
ready to take me, even as I am,
if I am willing
to find my way
down the stairs
and open myself
to life
once again.

The Poets

I came to hear the poets—
those whose words grace pages
and who live lives
deeper than mine—
hoping they will lead me
out of myself,
into another
world,
a parallel universe
where another version of me
lives and loves freely.

But I am only an amateur tracker
barely able to recognize wolf footprints.
I falter;
Second–guess myself.
I lose the tracks
that veer off
into uncharted terrain;
into the messy thicket
of life's underbrush,
where I sense the animal presence
hidden in the secret society
of those whose words grace pages.

I wonder if I will ever
become skillful and courageous enough
to follow the tracks
into that other world.

Afterwards, leaving Barnes and Noble,
walking into the light of the full moon,
I feel myself transforming,
Shape–shifting—
growing snout and tail;
spine bending at the hip;
arms becoming legs;
hands becoming paws;
fur sprouting over all
the years forgotten.
And I run,
wild,
into the shadows;
into the night;
into the thicket.

I already know
it will be gone
tomorrow—
a dream fragment
lingering somewhere
just outside of reach.
I already know
I must come again
to hear the poets;
let them point out
the wolf tracks
I won't recognize
as my own.

Finding Family

Those who tell us,
"you can never go home,"
do not know we have two families:
the family we were born into
and the family we create.

The family we were born into
cannot be given or taken
because it is between us and around us
forming a circle from the moment of conception
when one and one make three.

A force thicker than the blood we share binds us;
greater than the genes
that color our hair and our eyes,
that give us a part of our mother and father
and make us look alike as brother and sister.

While the family we create
can only be fashioned
through the giving and taking of ourselves over time
because it is inside us and runs through us
in all our moments together and apart.

A power greater than the promises
we make and break with each other
stitches our stories together
into a stronger fabric
that clothes us in storms
and decorates us in celebrations.

And our quest for finding family
will lead us back to the home in our hearts
where we create the family we are born into
and we are born again in the family we create.

Happy Feet

I have watched the dancers
move with a grace
I do not believe belongs to me.

It takes a drink
and a rock song
that does not require standard steps
before I get happy feet.

I blame it on a gimp leg.

But the real reason
lies in the heart of George Bailey
who watched the chipping away
of his dreams and desires
over the years
until he had none
burdened with responsibility
for the world in which
he grew up.

We get only glimpses
of his tortured soul
while his selfless purity
shines more brightly
than any human I have known,
especially myself.

No angel comes to show me
the effect of my absence.
No deaths prevented,
no careers saved,
no towns that would otherwise
sink into moral depravity.

George returns from tragedy
to embrace every particle of his life
down to the broken knob on the stairwell.

But I do not want to wait
for tragedy before
I learn to embrace life.
I want to dance
with my own hobbled grace
even if before judging eyes.
Let them carry the curse
of the broken knob
while angels earn their wings
on happy feet.

(Inspired by the classic movie, *It's a Wonderful Life*,
starring Jimmy Stewart as George Bailey)

Loving

Beauty

Beauty is not hidden
in empty rooms and broken hearts.

You simply do not see it.

Beauty is not lost
in lonely abandoned lots
covered over in weeds of regret.

You simply do not feel it.

Beauty is not absent
even in the discord that lives within you.

You simply do not hear it.

Beauty flowers inside
your suffering as well as your joy;
spreads a rainbow across your sadness,
blankets your night sky with stars,
and rises in you each morning
with the opening of your eyes.

For there is no beauty in the world
that is not within you.

And when you live beauty
from the inside out,
you will fall in love with the world
and be caressed
by every precious passing moment.

You will walk,
broken hearted,
into empty rooms
and dance to your own discord.

You will weed out regrets,
one by one,
from your own abandoned lots
making way for the flowering of you.

And you will return to the garden
you never left
and find beauty
waiting there;
all around you
        simply to be seen,
                to be felt,
                        to be heard.

Somewhere Between

I have lived my life
somewhere between
loneliness and love;
making the most
of the space,
root–bound,
in the little bit of soil
I allow myself.

Enough to live but not
enough to thrive.
Wanting more but not
willing to risk
the transplant
to unknown soil.

While
somewhere beneath
the surface of me,
little root–fingers
search slowly
for new ground—

pushing against the borders
and slipping through
all the holes and cracks—

reaching out
for the nutrients
found in loneliness
as well as love.
And then, beyond,
into the earth
to receive the nourishment
of life itself.

Salt Sea

Take these drops of the salt sea from my eyes.
Drain the ocean between us that flooded my empty heart
the moment I took wing and flew away from you.

Fill the darkness inside me
with stars from your heaven
and give me your full moon
that I may feel your presence
from the other side of daylight
half a world away.

Let the memory of your hand in mine,
walking through the garden,
be enough for now.

Please take these drops of the salt sea from my eyes;
fashion them into crystal earrings and wear me close to you
all the days we are apart.

Seeking

I have been seeking that place in my heart
I have kept for you through all these years,
like a little box filled with precious things
that mean nothing to others
and everything to oneself,
stored away somewhere for safekeeping
and hidden so well it has been concealed
even from myself.

A seeking that highlights the clutter of life
as a collection of trivia and distraction.

A seeking that signals a time for spring cleaning;
a time to attend to the feng shui of the heart.

Taking extra care with what I put there—
the placement of my passions and my pains;
the arrangement of what I hold dear.

Seeking the proper position
of each thing and each thought,
so the space speaks of what I live for
and why I move through life;
and opens up to make room for you again
and for the first time.

Seeking a spot for the little box of precious treasures—
a spot that serves as a centerpiece and a celebration
there in that place in my heart
I have kept for you through all these years;
that place that can be found only in a heart
broken open to love.

From Me

I send flowers and poetry,
travel across oceans to see you,
but I fear it is not enough.
I will never know what is left behind
when the poems are packed away
and the flowers wither
until I recognize your love
comes from you and not from me.

I have decided
I will sit in the temple
until I know what it is I love.
Words are not lost
in the house of spirit
though it only hears
what is said in the heart.

I will strip your charms from my ears.
I will strip your beauty from my eyes.
I will strip your body from my body.

I will go beyond words;
I will stay after flowers wither
until what is about you is about me
and what you suffer I suffer.
I will sit until I come to know
what it is I love
and say in my heart
my love comes from me
and not from you.

Migration

We sat perched upon a wall
overlooking the sea
where migrant birds
come to rest between worlds;
where teachers become students
and students become teachers.

You taught me Chinese greetings,
the names of fruits,
and what you call your dearest friends;
while I longed for the words to ask you
about tattooed memories of your first love
or how you mix fragrances into perfumes.
But there were not enough migrant words between us.

You taught me the colors I wear well—
the pale yellows and light oranges
found in the full moon rising
and I wanted to shine.
I wanted to hire you for shopping,
though we only had time
for shoelaces and a moon yellow shirt.

You taught me how to eat hairy crab—
the precise points to crack the shell
and where to find the tender meat.
And though I made a mess of it
with my hairy crab arms,
I felt my shell crack open
to something tender in me.

I wanted to tell you but I could only watch
words take wing and circle between worlds,
so many miles and so many years apart,
migrating across an ocean that touches both our shores
and coming to rest here in the heart
where there is no need to translate.

Love Remembers

Love remembers more
than pressed flowers
held precious
in the pages of a book;
more than moments
of lost innocence
captured long ago
on film.

Yet it travels
across the years,
closer than a heartbeat;
deeper than a secret wish.
Awakening itself again
in print and pictures,

it moves in you
like blood and breath
seeking an opening
to flood your being,
to fill the world with light
so that you may see again
what you are made of.

Blank Book
(for Yolanda)

In my hands, I hold
the blank book
you sent me.
I know poems will appear
on these empty pages
because they are already filled
with your love.

Each page opens itself
to the moment
it will give birth.
Words clamor to be written
in the space you have given me
to be myself.

A field of flowers
sprouts from seeds
that only need
a little soil and water
to be awakened.

I picked this moonflower for you
because it opens in the dark.
Its sweet fragrance deepens sleep
turning each night into a blank page
upon which you may write your dreams.

Dreams

Feed me your dreams
and I'll shine for you.

I'll swim through the clouds, surfacing heaven–side,
and deliver your wish to the Angels.
It is my purpose.

I clothed myself in flesh
and stepped upon the earth
for this reason, although
I've spent a lifetime denying it.

But I will no longer let fear rule the house of love.

Now, I hunger for your desire.
It's what powers the stars and turns the earth on its axis.
And it only asks to be believed.

It's too easy to hang dreams in heaven
and feel they are out of reach,
too easy to let our desires ferment
and forget we are making wine
for the celebration of life.

So, feed me your dreams
and I will shine for you.

Bone Knobby

Bone knobby hands,
bulging river veins,
speckled age spots.

500,000 hours worth
of skin deep secrets
holding stories
that may never be deciphered

of minutes and moments
that make up a life—

a history of grips and gripes
and tender touch;

of changing diapers
and doing dishes;

of writing and wronging
and giving and taking;

of handshakes and high–fives
and come–here's and stops;

of everything handled
and all out of reach—

molded by cooking and cutting
and cleaning and creating
and years forgetting her youth.

Yet still longing to be held
in the bone knobby hand
of the once again lover,
lost to her in all the middle years
of making money and raising children.

But his touch can still send a shiver
somewhere up the spine of her soul.

And you can see it
in the curl of her lips,
as his fingers encircle hers,

while their eyes look off
at separate horizons.

Give Us Wings

Nature is not always kind, but never cruel,
can be unforgiving, but is always loving.
The rose, one day whipped by the wind,
burnt by the sun, still accepts the morning dew.

Who are we to reject Grace
pointing to our flaws,
to claim the scars on our soul
justify hardening the heart?

And what lessons do we have to learn
when the eighty year old grandmother of 17,
the oldest at the party, is the first to dance;
when a crippled old man in purple pajamas
shows us what we gain cataloguing our handicaps
can never steal our joy?

So, let us give our gifts freely
looking each other in the eye and asking,
"Is it given from the bottom of the heart?"
because only the heart can give without conditions,
only the heart can receive Grace,
only the heart can teach us how
to free ourselves from the love that holds us in chains
in order to find the love that gives us wings.

Heaven

What is the world to me?
A tin cup in a beggar's hand
waiting to hear the "clink"
of every coin you drop.

What you discard as worthless
is worth more than years
because you teach me
that there is no gate to heaven.

 Love turns away no one.

The walls I see exist only inside my eyes,
the gate only inside my mind.

I was too busy laying claim to the world
to notice heaven around me;
too concerned with the coins in my cup
to realize I made myself a beggar in life.

Then, you came!
You believed in me.
Your eyes twinkling like stars
in the night sky
witnessing my dreams.
Your smile rising like the morning sun,
melting walls and gates and
awakening the magic in me.

How can I ever give to you
what you have given me?

I offer what I have with love.
I pour the wine of my words
into your cup, wanting us
to get drunk on life
and share the heaven in our hearts.

Already

My heart knew you
before
you arrived
in my life.

The shape of you
already
lived within me.

Your voice was
already
whispering
in my soul
as if you were
a part of me.

There were no fireworks
or thunderbolts
when you arrived.

You came
like another gentle wave
upon my shore

as if
you had already arrived
a million times before;

as if
our sea and shore
had been dancing
since before memories,

before eyes
witnessed
beauty in the world;

as if
you had always
been there,

the candle
I kept lit
in the window,

the light
to bring home
the one true love
lost to the world.

Thank You

I want to thank you
        because I am falling in love with you
        and this has awakened something in me
        that is at once
            very beautiful,
                very powerful,
                    and very frightening.

It has opened me to being touched by you
        on a very deep level.
It has opened me to seeing in you
        the face of the beloved.
It has opened me to hearing you
        calling me back,
            and back again,
                to that wellspring of poetry and passion.

And even though I weave a world with you in it
        from memories
            and fantasies
                and moments yet to be,

I want you to know that I will always respect your boundaries
        and I will respect my own boundaries
            as I navigate to discover
            what it means in my life
            to be turning myself over to love
                without yet knowing
                    where it will go…

Notes

Money

I wrote this poem while attending a Wealthy Mind Trainer's Training taught by my good friends Tim and Kris Hallbom in 2004. Money is a powerful symbol and often bears the burden of our dreams and desires as well as our fears and failures. Tim and Kris have found that most people struggle in relationship to money, which serves as a doorway to identifying limiting beliefs that interfere with living life on our own terms.

Sky in a Jar

I wrote a series of poems about poets inspired by hearing poets read their own work at poetry readings. " Sky In a Jar" was written after hearing Hannah Stein read her poetry at Barnes and Noble Sacramento on 2/19/03. Several images from her reading lingered in my mind and a poem of my own emerged. I was especially moved by the phrase "sky in a jar" and by her poem "Zoo Vigil" describing zoo animals mourning the dead. Another of her poems referenced plate tectonics and her final poem praised the sensuous delights of blackberries.

Moon Lake

This poem is dedicated to the students of the May 2007 Shanghai Hypnotherapy Training Program. One student described a wrenching conflict between two seemingly incompatible goals and how she shopped for shoes as a distraction. Conflict and distraction became a theme for the class, including how easy it is to set our sights on something external rather than finding fulfillment within.

Cup of Life

This poem emerged from the feeling of overwhelm that I have felt and many of my clients and students have reported over the years. It also comes from a sense of my mother, a consummate worrier, trying to protect my siblings and me from the onslaught of life. One day I awoke with an image of Mom standing in front of us at a beach, arms outstretched, trying to block an oncoming tidal wave. That image served as the backdrop for "Cup of Life."

The Reservoir of Sadness

I attended a training program on Ericksonian Hypnotherapy with a small group of fellow students at Esalen Institute taught by Paul Lounsbury and Nancy Winston around 2004. This poem emerged from images and input shared by fellow students. One attendee told of falling into a coma (not metaphorically—an actual coma) for a few weeks prior to the class. I don't recall what caused the coma, but I do recall the vivid sense of being absent from one's own life. Another student talked of a vast sadness, which became our theme as a group during the week together.

The White Stick

I composed this poem while watching our driver smoke beside the van as we waited in line at the customs station in Shenzhen Bay border between Shenzhen and Hong Kong. Over the years, I have watched and heard people who smoke express a love–hate relationship with cigarettes. Their "relationship" to cigarettes seems to reflect a strange intimacy with something that slowly steals your life as it did with my father, who died from lung cancer in 1996.

Struggling to Relax

A student in a hypnotherapy class said he was "struggling to relax" and this comment provided the title and theme for this poem. At times, many people, myself included, face this irony of working hard to relax. Our bodies become accustomed to tension and we hold tightened muscles unconsciously. The unnatural tension becomes natural. Consequently, we must work at relaxing and struggle against what has become normal in our bodies.

Down to the Bone

I wrote this poem while in the process of divorce and cleaning out 20 years of accumulating things from my life. It seemed almost unending. Each time I thought I arrived at the end, there was another box or another closet to go through and take the remnants to the nearest Goodwill, the American icon of charity. It was a heart–wrenching act of letting go of the life I had lived in order to find something deeper in myself.

Fate

In my classes, I often listen for themes from content shared by students and images presented in class to serve as poetic sources. This poem evolved out of the themes and images offered by students in the June 2009 Hypnotherapy class in Chengdu, China.

The Poets

Barnes and Noble bookstore at Arden Fair Mall in Sacramento hosted periodic poetry readings in 2002–4 and I attended many of these events. One evening, probably in 2002, two poets shared the floor and served as the inspiration for this poem, which came almost whole while driving home. Unfortunately, I neglected to write down these poets' names. One of these poets, I believe it was Dennis Schmitz, shared a poem about tracking wolves and the other, I think it may have been Jose Montoya, shared several earthy, gritty poems that expressed, to me, living life wild and raw.

Sacred Relics

The Art of Pilgrimage: The Seeker's Guide to Making Travel Sacred by Phil Cousineau served as inspiration for "Sacred Relics." Cousineau encourages a view of travel and of life as a sacred act and an honoring of your own spiritual journey. To me, it highlighted a sense of having two selves: one lives a surface life of habits and hobbies, interests and interactions on a daily basis; and a second, of which I am only faintly aware, lives on a deeper, richer level. Every once in a while I feel that second self beckoning me, inviting me, to step into that other life, though I fear I will lose the first life in the process.

Twists and Turns

I composed "Twists and Turns" at the last weekend of the "Healing the Light Body" training program with Alberto Villoldo and the Four Winds Society as my expression of gratitude to Alberto and his staff.

Happy Feet

Most people will recognize the character of George Bailey from the classic movie *It's a Wonderful Life* as the inspiration for this poem. George Bailey epitomizes the self–sacrifice many people, especially parents, choose by putting duty before desire. The movie is a classic reframe of regret into gratitude and invites you, as the viewer, to embrace the life you live just as it is.

Migration

This poem is dedicated to Jenny Lee and commemorates the day we spent together on my day off during my second visit to Shenzhen in 2005.

Give Us Wings

This poem is dedicated to Juan Ramirez Martinez, better known as Paco, and to his family, the staff of CMPNL, and the presenters and students at the CMPNL 20th Anniversary Congress in Guadalajara, October, 2008. The week–long congress focused on three primary topics taught at CMPNL: NLP, Hypnotherapy, and Coaching. The eighty–year–old grandmother is Paco's mother and the man in purple pajamas refers to Milton H. Erickson. I taught a class on emotional debt during the congress and a student shared the idea that only those things offered from the "bottom of the heart" are given without conditions.

Heaven

"Heaven" is another poem inspired by a student in a hypnotherapy class, who described how her uncle believed in her during a difficult time and this became a powerful transition point and reference experience in her life. Her description resonated with my own experience of being encouraged to teach NLP by my first NLP teacher, Richard Clarke. I also feel a strong sense that students in my classes believe in me. I often tell students that a teacher is made great not by his or her own greatness, but by the students who bring out the greatness in the teacher. Hence, this poem is dedicated to all the students who have believed in me as a teacher and mentor over the years. They give to me more than I can ever give to them.

Acknowledgements

Cultivating the poetic craft is not a common path and many fellow poets walk this road alone, often solely for their own self–expression. Some closet poets rarely share their work because it may seem hard to find appreciative ears. I have been blessed to have captive audiences at my seminars around the world and have subjected learners to poetry readings that I thought fit a theme or supported a message.

I feel deeply grateful for the many students who have come to me after a reading to say the poem touched them in some way and who have urged me to publish my work. I assured them that I would, but admit that it has, for many of these supporters, taken me years to follow through on my word. I hope this work not only realizes that promise, but also proves to be worth the wait and satisfies the deeper expectation behind their request.

There is a long list of people who have supported me, directly and indirectly, some knowingly and others unknowingly, in my journey to become a poet and consequently to the realization of this book. I want to thank Robert Evans and the Full Time Messenger mastermind group, who gave me the title and urged me to step into my identity as the "transformational poet." Much love goes to Max Simon for his "steel wall" coaching and the Enlightened Entrepreneur Club mastermind group, who opened my eyes to the power of my poetry in helping others "sing the unsung song."

A special thanks goes to Tim and Kris Hallbom, the best friends a person could have, who have done so much for my career as a trainer, which provided a platform for sharing my poetry over the years. Thanks also to the many sponsors who have invited me to teach and allowed me to share poetry despite the topic, including Juan Ramirez (Paco) in Guadalajara, Mexico;

Oscar Ramirez in Monterrey, Mexico; Monica Azcarate in Mexico City; Kay Reis in Seattle; Marilou Seavey in Boston; Susan Stageman in Dallas; Helen Attridge Green in Northern California; Bruce Winner with LRCCD and programs throughout California; Roberta Faddoul in Australia; Leeane Ooi in Malaysia; Ruth Wang in Malaysia; Jessica So in Hong Kong; Valent Lee in China; Liu Tao and the HRI network in China; and Clement Thai in China. Thanks also to Jenny Lee, who helped me negotiate some of the ways of China, many so strange to the Western mind, and who also taught me so much about myself along the way. A special thanks goes to my translator and business partner in China, RongJing (Ellen) whose translations consistently hit the mark and who has done so much to open the Chinese ear to my poetic expression.

My nomadic lifestyle would certainly be much more difficult to sustain were it not for the incredible generosity of my brother, Don, who cares for my home while I travel to exotic places. He has always been a model for me. Thanks also to my sister, Teri, who has always made me feel she is proud of me and that is a true gift to one who lives outside the norm in life. And the deepest thank you to my Mother, Vida, who passed away in October, 2011. Vida means "beloved" in Hebrew and "life" in Spanish and she truly blessed me with this beloved life.

Many people inspired individual poems and I have made some notes in the book about the sources in some cases. A special thanks goes to Mary Valtierra, who was my partner for many years and provided the fertilizer for the landscape of my soul, the source from which many poems sprouted. Although I may not specify whom in my notes, some specific people inspired specific poems. For those in this group, these poems are my way of sharing the heaven in my heart with you. Many poems came directly out of classes or from personal experiences with groups and some came from unknowing strangers who served as projections for my own unfolding wisdom. I am grateful to all those who served to inspire me. I hope these poems inspire those who inspired me to find the heaven in their hearts.

I also want to thank all those who contributed to the work itself. Justin Bancroft and Tarja Stoeckl provided support for my business and Internet structure, some help with social media (a world I have yet to master), and editing input on the manuscript itself. Thanks also to Terry and Marcia Fieland, who helped transform it into a publishable product. Lastly, thanks to the team at 99Designs for providing a great method to get the cover design.

Nick LeForce

About the Author

As mentioned in the introduction, I have been a part–time poet for most of my life because I let the Muse take the lead and she comes and goes as she pleases. Though she is wild, she requires discipline from her disciples, a trait I admittedly lack. So, it has taken years for me to step into my identity as a poet and, only recently, actually stand before my classes and declare, "I am a poet."

I am otherwise occupied as a life coach and trainer of NLP (Neuro–Linguistic Programming) and Hypnotherapy offering programs in the US, Mexico, Australia, Malaysia, China and elsewhere. I have been privileged to offer on–site consulting and training programs to businesses working with both public and private sector clients, including AT&T, Blue Diamond Almond Growers, California Department of Fish and Game, California Department of General Services, California Farm Bureau Federation, California State Teachers Retirement System, California Water Resources Control Board, Citizens Utilities, Holiday Inn, Management Recruiters International, Merchant Bank of China, Pepsico International, Prudential Insurance, Sacramento County Municipal Services Agency, Sacramento County Planning Agency, SBC Communications, Sheraton Hotels, Standard Office Systems, United Corporate Furnishings, Varsity Contractors, York & Associates Law Firm and others. I am also a faculty member of the Los Rios Community College District in Sacramento, CA.

Sharing poetry at these events had become a signature aspect of my work, but the reading was only a support for a topic and no more than one poem per day at the most. Recently, I have boldly began to integrate poems into classes more extensively, using them to make teaching points or as stimuli for exercises and activities. I have made a stand with my sponsors that I will be using poetry as a primary tool in my classes because it is in these readings that I feel most aligned with my message and most impactful in my teaching with students.

This book is a collection of selected works from seven little books of poetry I had previously printed up for friends and family and occasionally made available at classes. I have also authored several books, including *I Owe You, You Owe Me: Breaking the shackles of emotional debt and creating abundant relationships,* (2006); *Coaching in the Workplace: A pocket guide of strategies and tools for powerful change,* (2008); and *Co–Creation: How to collaborate for results,* (2009).

Please follow me on Twitter (nickleforce), friend with me on Facebook (www.facebook.nick.leforce), or visit my website at www.transformationalpoet.com.